GILGAMESH

GILGAMESH

A New Rendering

in English Verse

■

David Ferry

Farrar, Straus and Giroux

New York

■

811.
54
Ferry

Library of Congress catalog card number 92-71534

Tablets I–V first appeared in TriQuarterly, a publication of
Northwestern University, No. 83 (February 1992). Part of Tablet
VI first appeared in Partisan Review, LIX, No. 2 (Spring
1992). Tablets VII–IX first appeared in Raritan: A Quarterly
Review, XI, No. 4 (Spring 1992). Tablets X–XI first appeared
in Arion: A Journal of Humanities and the Classics, at
Boston University, Third Series, I, No. 3 (Fall 1991).

ACKNOWLEDGMENTS
I want to thank the editors at Farrar, Straus & Giroux, especially
Elisheva Urbas, and the designer, Cynthia Krupat. I am grateful
for the advice and encouragement I have received from many
friends and colleagues. I especially thank my wife, Anne Ferry, and
also Frank Bidart and Robert Pinsky, friends in the art, Dimitri
Hadzi, and William L. Moran.

This book is dedicated to Suzie and Bill

CONTENTS

INTRODUCTION

According to Sumerian tradition, Gilgamesh was an early ruler of the city-state of Uruk, biblical Erech, and the evidence, admittedly meager and indirect, puts him there around the twenty-seventh century B.C.E. Of his actual achievements we know nothing except what is perhaps reflected in the later traditions of him as heroic warrior and builder of his city's mighty walls.

For the Sumerians, and later for the Assyrians and Babylonians, Gilgamesh was both god and hero. As the former, he appears in a god-list about a century after his death, and he continued to be worshipped for another two thousand years, until the end of the Assyro-Babylonian civilization. He was an underworld deity, a judge there and sometimes called its king. His statues or figurines appear in burial rites for the dead, and his cult was especially important in the month of Ab (July–August), when nature itself, as it were, expired.

As hero, Gilgamesh undoubtedly lived on in the oral traditions of the Sumerians, especially at the court of Uruk. When these traditions were first committed to writing is not known. The earliest compositions we have, five or six, probably do not go back further than the late third millennium B.C.E. Though they are sometimes poorly preserved, we can identify in them themes and tales that will later be integrated in the Babylonian epic. Thus, in one lay, we find Gilgamesh, along with Enkidu and other retainers, striving to achieve the immortality of fame by the slaying of the monster Huwawa (see below, Tablets

IV–V). In another, we read of the royal oppression of Uruk (see below, Tablet I). In another, the goddess Inanna unleashes the Bull of Heaven upon Gilgamesh and Enkidu (see below, Tablet VI). In still others, Enkidu is trapped and must remain in the underworld (see below, Tablets VII–VIII), and Gilgamesh resents his own mortality (see below, Tablets IX–XI).

These compositions in Sumerian, or similar ones, written or oral, in the Sumerian or the Babylonian languages, were the sources for the Babylonian composition that followed in the early second millennium B.C.E., what is known as the Old Babylonian period. This epic is not a translation of a Sumerian original. It is, rather, a highly selective and creative adaptation and transformation of what we find in the earlier works. It is still known only in fragments, but it was certainly a work of at least one thousand lines, perhaps much longer, focused on a central theme, man's mortality. It begins with Gilgamesh's exhausting his people with the labors of the corvée and introduces a very new Enkidu, not the retainer of the Sumerian tradition, but a hairy Wild Man, created by the gods to match Gilgamesh's enormous energies, eventually humanized, and Gilgamesh's beloved friend and companion in his adventures. He joins Gilgamesh in his quest for the immortality of fame, an old Sumerian theme, but then the text goes its own highly original way: Enkidu is punished for his part in the death of Huwawa and dies. Consumed with grief, Gilgamesh reacts by rejecting the heroic ideals of the past and, in effect, rejects his humanity. He will be content now only with the true immortality of the gods. He therefore journeys to the end of the world to find the one immortal man, the Babylonian Noah, Utnapishtim, and to learn from him the secret of his unending life.

In the centuries that followed, knowledge of the epic spread across the ancient Near East, not only in its Babylonian form but also in versions written in the Elamite, Hittite, and Hurrian languages. Recent discoveries indicate that the epic had assumed more or less its standard form by the thirteenth century B.C.E. The standard version of eleven tablets (with a twelfth as an appendix, a later and poorly integrated addition and, unlike the rest of the epic, a literal translation into Babylonian from a Sumerian original) is a work of about three thousand lines and is known mainly from the Nineveh recension on tablets of the seventh century B.C.E. Babylonian tradition credited it to a poet-editor by the name of Sin-leqe-unninni, "Sin (the moon god), accept my plea."

It is this relatively late, standard text, with occasional assistance from the Old Babylonian version, that is the basis of the poem by David Ferry that follows. And let it be stated at once: it is David Ferry's poem. It is not Sin-leqe-unninni's or anyone else's, any more than *The Vanity of Human Wishes* is Juvenal's and not Johnson's. He has given us, not a translation, not at least as that term is ordinarily understood, but a transformation. He does not compete, therefore, with the earlier translators, whose contribution to his own work he generously acknowledges, nor should his work be compared with theirs. He has given us what they have not and what as authors of word-for-word translations they could not aspire to. He has given us a work of verbal art. He has thereby communicated to us some sense of the beauty of the original and some sense of the emotions that reading or hearing the original must have aroused. In this respect, however free his version on one level may be, on another and deeper one it seems remarkably faithful to the original. It is, therefore, a major contribution to our understanding and appreciation of this ancient and moving poem.

WILLIAM L. MORAN
the Andrew W. Mellon Professor of the Humanities,
Emeritus, Harvard University
Brunswick, Maine

GILGAMESH

i

The Story

of him who knew the most of all men know;
who made the journey; heartbroken; reconciled;

who knew the way things were before the Flood,
the secret things, the mystery; who went

to the end of the earth, and over; who returned,
and wrote the story on a tablet of stone.

He built Uruk. He built the keeping place
of Anu and Ishtar. The outer wall

shines in the sun like brightest copper; the inner
wall is beyond the imagining of kings.

Study the brickwork, study the fortification;
climb the great ancient staircase to the terrace;

study how it is made; from the terrace see
the planted and fallow fields, the ponds and orchards.

This is Uruk, the city of Gilgamesh
the Wild Ox, son of Lugalbanda, son

of the Lady Wildcow Ninsun, Gilgamesh
the vanguard and the rear guard of the army,

Shadow of Darkness over the enemy field,
the Web, the Flood that rises to wash away

the walls of alien cities, Gilgamesh
the strongest one of all, the perfect, the terror.

It is he who opened passes through the mountains;
and he who dug deep wells on the mountainsides;

who measured the world; and sought out Utnapishtim
beyond the world; it is he who restored the shrines;

two-thirds a god, one-third a man, the king.
Go to the temple of Anu and Ishtar:

open the copper chest with the iron locks;
the tablet of lapis lazuli tells the story.

ii

There was no withstanding the aura or power of the Wild
Ox Gilgamesh. Neither the father's son

nor the wife of the noble; neither the mother's daughter
nor the warrior's bride was safe. The old men said:

"Is this the shepherd of the people? Is this
the wise shepherd, protector of the people?"

The gods of heaven listened to their complaint.
"Aruru is the maker of this king.

4

Neither the father's son nor the wife of the noble
is safe in Uruk; neither the mother's daughter

nor the warrior's bride is safe. The old men say:
'Is this the shepherd of the people? Is this

the wise shepherd, protector of the people?
There is no withstanding the desire of the Wild Ox.' "

They called the goddess Aruru, saying to her:
"You made this man. Now create another.

Create his double and let the two contend.
Let stormy heart contend with stormy heart

that peace may come to Uruk once again."
Aruru listened and heard and then created

out of earth clay and divine spittle the double,
the stormy-hearted other, Enkidu,

the hairy-bodied wild man of the grasslands,
powerful as Ninurta the god of war,

the hair of his head like the grain fields of the goddess,
naked as Sumuqan the god of cattle.

He feeds upon the grasslands with gazelles;
visits the watering places with the creatures

whose hearts delight, as his delights, in water.

One day a hunter came to a watering place
and *saw* Enkidu; he stood expressionless,

astonished; then with his silent dogs he went
home to his father's house, fear in his belly.

His face was as one estranged from what he knows.
He opened his mouth and said to his father: "Father,

I saw a hairy-bodied man today
at the watering place, powerful as Ninurta

the god of war; he feeds upon the grasslands
with gazelles; he visits the watering places

with the beasts; he has unset my traps and filled
my hunting pits; the creatures of the grasslands

get away free. The wild man sets them free.
Because of him I am no longer a hunter."

His father said: "Go to Uruk and there
present yourself to Gilgamesh the king,

who is the strongest of all, the perfect, the terror,
the wise shepherd, protector of the people.

Tell him about the power of the wild man.
Ask him to send a harlot back with you,

a temple prostitute, to conquer him
with her greater power. When he visits the watering place,

let her show him her breasts, her beauty, for his wonder.
He will lie with her in pleasure, and then the creatures,

the gazelles with whom he feeds upon the grasslands,
and the others with whom he visits the watering places,

will flee from him who ranged the hills with them."
So the hunter went to Gilgamesh in Uruk

and told him about the power of the wild man,
and how he had unset the traps and filled

the pits, so that the creatures got away free.
The lord of Uruk said to the hunter then:

"When you return, a temple prostitute
will go with you and with her beauty conquer

the wild man. He will lie with her and then
the gazelles with whom he feeds upon the grasslands,

and the others with whom he visits the watering places,
will flee from him who ranged the hills with them."

iv

The harlot and the hunter traveled together,
taking three days, back to the watering place.

For three more days they waited, and finally
Enkidu came with the creatures that love the water,

the gazelles and the others, so as to drink their fill.
The temple prostitute looked at him, Enkidu,

the hairy-bodied wild man of the grasslands,
the hair of his head like the grain fields of the goddess,

naked as Sumuqan the god of cattle.
"That is Enkidu, Shamhat, show him your breasts,

show him your beauty. Spread out your cloak on the ground.
Lie down on it. The wild man will look at you.

Show him your body. The hairy-bodied man
will come to you and lie down on you; and then

show him the things a woman knows how to do.
The gazelles and with them all the other creatures

will flee from him who ranged the hills with them."
And so the harlot, Shamhat, showed him her breasts,

showed him her body. The hairy-bodied man
came over to her, and lay down on her, and then

she showed him the things a woman knows how to do.
For seven days Enkidu in his wonder

lay with her in pleasure, and then at last
went to seek out the company of the creatures

whose hearts delight in feeding upon the grasslands,
and visiting the watering places, and

ranging the hills. But seeing him, they fled.
The creatures were gone, and everything was changed.

His body that loved to range the hills was now
unable to follow; but in the mind of the wild man

there was beginning a new understanding.
Bewildered, he turned, and sought out the company

of the temple prostitute. He sat down beside her,
and looked into her face, and listened to her:

"Enkidu, now you are beautiful as a god.
Why do you seek the company of beasts?

Come with me to the city, to Uruk,
to the temple of Anu and the goddess Ishtar.

Gilgamesh is the ruler, the strongest of all,
the terror. The aura and power of his desire

can be withstood by no one." Then Enkidu,
whose heart was beginning to know about itself

and longed for a companion, cried aloud:
"Take me to Uruk, the city of Gilgamesh,

whose aura and power cannot be withstood.
I will cry out in Uruk, challenging him:

'It is I, Enkidu. The strength of the wild man
born in the wilderness cannot be withstood.'"

The temple prostitute replied: "Come then
to Uruk, where the processions are, and music,

and let us go together through the dancing
to the palace hall where Gilgamesh presides,

the favorite of the gods, the beautiful,
strongest of all, the terror, the most desired.

Look at his radiant face, the favorite
of Shamash and Enlil, Ea, and Anu.

While you were grazing beastlike with gazelles,
before your mind had any understanding,

his mind, a gift to the gifted of the gods,
had a dream of you before you knew of him.

In the early morning Gilgamesh arose
and told his mother his dream: 'I had a dream.

A star fell from the heavens, a meteorite,
and lay on the empty plain outside Uruk.

The men and women came and wondered at it.
I strove with it to lift it but could not.

I was drawn to it as if it was a woman.'
All-knowing Rimat-Ninsun spoke to him,

the lord of Uruk, Gilgamesh. His mother,
All-knowing Rimat-Ninsun, spoke and said:

'The star that fell from the heavens, the meteorite
that lay on the empty plain outside Uruk,

the star you could not lift when you strove with it,
the star you were drawn to as if drawn to a woman,

is the strong companion, powerful as a star,
the meteorite of the heavens, a gift of the gods.

That you were drawn to it as if drawn to a woman
means that this companion will not forsake you.

He will protect and guard you with his life.
This is the fortunate meaning of your dream.'

Then Gilgamesh the lord of Uruk said:
'May the dream as you interpret come to pass.' "

The temple prostitute thus told the tale.

i

Shamhat took off her robe and divided it
so that the wild man also could be clothed.

When this was done and both of them were clothed,
she took him by the hand as a goddess might,

leading a worshipper into the temple precinct;
as if he was a child she held his hand

and they began their journey. They came to a camp
where shepherds lived, who gathered about and wondered

at the huge size and strength of Enkidu,
the hairy-bodied wild man of the grasslands.

They said to each other: "He is like Gilgamesh,
twice the size of ordinary men,

stronger and taller than a battlement.
He is like a star that has fallen from the heavens."

They cooked food and set it down before him;
they brought out beer they had brewed and set it down.

But Enkidu knew nothing about these things,
so he sat and stared at the cooked food and the beer

for a very long time, not knowing what to do.
Then Shamhat, the harlot, the temple prostitute,

said: "Enkidu, this is the food and drink
men eat and drink. Eat and drink your fill."

So Enkidu ate his fill of the cooked food,
and drank the beer. Seven jugs of the beer

and he was suddenly joyful, and sang aloud.
Then he washed his hairy body, anointed himself

with oil, and dressed his body in new clothes,
so that he looked as beautiful as a bridegroom.

He took up a weapon to guard the flocks and shepherds
against the wolves and lions that preyed upon them.

Therefore, at night, with Enkidu to guard them,
the shepherds could lie down in peaceful sleep.

ii

One day a stranger came into the camp
bearing a richly decorated platter,

and Enkidu asked Shamhat to question him.
"Where are you going? Where are you hurrying to?"

The young man opened his mouth and said to them:
"I am going to the wedding feast in Uruk,

bearing delicious offerings on the platter,
ceremonial offerings for the feast.

Before the husband, Gilgamesh will lie
in pleasure with the bride in the marital chamber.

There is no withstanding the aura or power of the desire
of the Wild Ox Gilgamesh, the strongest of all."

Then Enkidu was full of anger and said:
"Take me to Uruk, the city of Gilgamesh,

whose aura and power cannot be withstood.
I will cry out in Uruk, challenging him:

'It is I, Enkidu. The strength of the wild man
born in the wilderness cannot be withstood.'"

So they set out for the wedding feast in Uruk.

iii

Enkidu entered Uruk; then, amazement
crowded the streets at the sight of the size of him,

the strength and beauty, the likeness to Gilgamesh.
"One has appeared worthy of Gilgamesh,

stormy heart to struggle with stormy heart."
"The wedding feast of the goddess of love is ready."

Enkidu stood, guardian on the threshold
of the marital chamber, to block the way of the king,

the aura and power of the Wild Ox Gilgamesh,
who was coming to the chamber to take the bride.

Stormy heart struggled with stormy heart
as Gilgamesh met Enkidu in his rage.

At the marital threshold they wrestled, bulls contending;
the doorposts shook and shattered; the wrestling staggered,

wild bulls locked-horned and staggering staggered wrestling
through the city streets; the city walls and lintels

shuddered and swayed, the gates of the city trembled
as Gilgamesh, the strongest of all, the terror,

wrestled the wild man Enkidu to his knees.
And then the rage of Gilgamesh subsided.

He turned his chest away. Enkidu said:
"You are the strongest of all, the perfect, the terror.

The Lady Wildcow Ninsun bore no other.
Enlil has made you sovereign over the city."

Then Enkidu and Gilgamesh embraced,
and kissed, and took each other by the hand.

iv

Enkidu listened as Rimat-Ninsun spoke
to Gilgamesh her son: "Enkidu has neither

father nor mother; there is no one to cut
the wild man's hair. He was born on the grasslands and grazed

with gazelles and the other beasts on the grass of the grasslands;
Enkidu, the companion, will not forsake you."

.

Enkidu listened, and wept, and felt his weakness.
Then Enkidu and Gilgamesh embraced,

and kissed, and took each other by the hand.

Enkidu spoke these words to Gilgamesh:
"Huwawa's mouth is fire; his roar the floodwater;

his breath is death. Enlil made him guardian
of the Cedar Forest, to frighten off the mortal

who would venture there. But who would venture
there? Huwawa's mouth is fire; his roar

is the floodwater; he breathes and there is death.
He hears the slightest sound somewhere in the Forest.

Enlil made him terrifying guardian,
whose mouth is fire, whose roar the floodwater.

Helpless is he who enters the Cedar Forest."
But Gilgamesh replied: "Who is the mortal

able to enter heaven? Only the gods
can live forever. The life of man is short.

What he accomplishes is but the wind.
Where is the courage that you used to have?

Where is the strength? It is Gilgamesh
who will venture first into the Cedar Forest,

and you can follow after, crying out:
'Go on, go forward, go on, embrace the danger!'

You who have fought with lions and with wolves,
you know what danger is. Where is your courage?

If I should fall, my fame will be secure.
'It was Gilgamesh who fought against Huwawa!'

It is Gilgamesh who will venture into the Forest
and cut the Cedar down and win the glory.

My fame will be secure to all my sons."

vi

So the two warriors went to the armor makers,
who made them weapons as they watched them work,

axes, and swords, and adzes, weighty and mighty,
making each of them ready for the adventure.

The people gathered at the Seven-Bolt Gate,
and Gilgamesh, the king of Uruk, said:

"It is Gilgamesh who will venture into the Forest
and cut the Cedar down and win the glory.

My fame will be secure to all my sons.
The journey I will undergo has never

been undergone before. Give me your blessing.
I will return to celebrate the feast

of the New Year. Uruk will shout in praise."
The old men of the city said to him:

"Gilgamesh the king is a young man. His valiant
heart is restless and does not know its danger.

Huwawa's mouth is fire; his roar is the roar
of the floodwater; he breathes and there is death.

Helpless is he who enters the Cedar Forest."
Gilgamesh, the king of Uruk, said:

"It is Gilgamesh who will venture into the Forest."
The old men said: "Though you are strongest of all,

do not put all your trust in your own strength.
Let Enkidu, who knows the way to the Forest,

who knows the wilderness, let him go first.
Enkidu the companion will not forsake you.

Let him go first to find the way through the passes.
Let him whose heart delights in water find

the hidden wilderness places where the cold
pure secret of the earth may be disclosed

to quench your thirst. Offer to Shamash water.
May the god Shamash grant you your desire.

Be mindful of your father, Lugalbanda.
Be mindful of his memory. May he protect you."

Then Enkidu spoke and said to Gilgamesh:
"It is your restless heart's desire to venture

into the Cedar Forest. Enkidu
the companion will not forsake you. Let Enkidu,

who knows the wilderness, and knows the way
to the Cedar Forest, let Enkidu go first

to find the way through the passes and find the water
to quench your thirst and offer to the god."

vii

Then Gilgamesh and Enkidu together
went to the palace, Egalmah, to Ninsun

the All-knowing, mother of Gilgamesh.
Gilgamesh told his mother about the adventure,

how it is Gilgamesh who would kill Huwawa,
and cut the Cedar down and win the glory.

Ninsun listened grieving to what he said,
and then went grieving to her chamber where

she purified herself and put on garments
suitable to her task, and sprinkled ritual

water on the ground. She mounted the stairs
to the palace roof and at the altar burned

and offered offerings of plants, fragrant
and sacred, to propitiate the god:

"Why have you given my son a restless heart?
No one has ever undergone the journey

that he will undergo. Huwawa's mouth
is fire. O Shamash, my son Gilgamesh

is going to the Forest on your errand,
to kill the demon hateful to the sun god.

When Shamash sees him setting out on the road,
or in the mountain passes, or entering

the Forest, may Shamash guard and keep him safe.
And may the stars, the watchmen of the night,

watch over Gilgamesh and the companion."
Rimat-Ninsun, the mother of Gilgamesh,

in the company of the votaries of the temple,
spoke and said to Enkidu the companion,

placing a sacred pendant about his neck:
"Though not my son, here I adopt you son,

not to forsake my son in the future danger."
Then from the Seven-Bolt Gate the two departed,

hearing the warnings and blessings of the city.

TABLETS IV AND V

i

The two of them traveled fifty leagues a day,
never resting except at night trying

to rest, stopping only once a day to eat;
in three days' walk a hundred and fifty leagues,

a three weeks' walk for an ordinary man.
The third day Enkidu found the hidden water

to quench their thirst and offer to the god.
They dug a well and drank their fill and offered

a libation to the god. Then Gilgamesh
climbed to a high place on the mountainside

and offered the god an offering of flour:
"May the mountain bring a fortunate dream from Shamash."

They made camp there that night and Enkidu
prepared a sleeping place, prepared a shelter

against the wind that blew along the mountain.
The two of them sheltered themselves against the wind.

After a time the oblivion of sleep
poured in upon the king, the strongest of all.

He slept, but at midnight suddenly awoke,
and awakened the companion, Enkidu:

"Did you call out to me, just now, in the night?
Why did I waken? Was it you that touched me?

Was it a god went through the camp? A dream?
What makes my skin creep? I had a dream.

I dreamed we were going through a mountain gorge
and the huge mountain fell down on the two of us.

We were as little as flies compared to the mountain."
Enkidu, born in the wilderness, replied:

"The dream you dreamed tonight is fortunate.
The mountain that you dreamed about is Huwawa.

Huwawa will fall down like a mountain and die.
His dead body will lie on the plain like a mountain."

On the next day they traveled fifty leagues,
and fifty leagues a day for two days more.

Then Enkidu found the water. They dug a well
to quench their thirst and offer to the god,

and Gilgamesh offered his offering of flour:
"May Shamash grant a fortunate dream tonight."

Enkidu, born in the wilderness, made a shelter.
The two of them sheltered themselves against the wind.

After a time the oblivion of sleep
poured in upon the king. He fell asleep,

but at midnight suddenly woke up, disturbed,
and said to the companion, Enkidu:

"Did you call out to me in the night? Was it you
that touched me? Was it a god went through the camp?

In the dream I had, a great bull head was thrashing
over my body in glory, and bellowing

over me, me helpless on the ground; the breath
of the bull snout breathed on me; the bellowing

bull noise shook the earth and broke it open;
the choking dust rose up and filled the dream.

Then one brought water to me in my dream."
"The dream you dreamed tonight is fortunate.

The bull you dreamed of in your dream is not
the demon enemy guardian of the Forest.

The bull is Shamash. The wrestling is his blessing.
The one who brought you water is your father."

On the next day they traveled fifty leagues,
in three days' time one hundred and fifty leagues,

a three weeks' walk for an ordinary man.
Then Enkidu found the place to dig a well

to quench their thirst and offer to the god,
and Gilgamesh made his offering of flour:

"May Shamash grant a fortunate dream tonight."
Enkidu, born in the wilderness, made a shelter.

The two of them sheltered themselves against the wind
and a shower of rain that passed across the mountain.

After a time the oblivion of sleep
poured in upon the king. He slept, but at midnight

suddenly awoke, and said to the companion:
"Did you call out to me, just now, in the night?

Why did I waken? Was it you that touched me?
Was it a god went through the camp? A dream?

What makes me fearful? I had a dream.
The earth shook and the sky shook; and a white glare

filled up the sky, and then there was nothing at all
but silence and darkness, and after that the lightning

broke out and the thunder everywhere, and then
the rain was fire that was raining down,

and then the rain was ashes raining down.
Let us go back from the mountain, down to the plain.

Let us consider all these things together."
But Enkidu once again told Gilgamesh

that the dream he had dreamed that night was fortunate.
So day after day they journeyed on to the Forest.

There were other dreams that disturbed the sleep of the king,
night after night as they journeyed to the Forest,

and Enkidu always said they were fortunate.
Gilgamesh, weeping, prayed to the god Shamash:

"Be mindful of the promise asked in Uruk.
Guard and protect those who go on your errand,

to kill the demon hateful to the god.
Protect us as we pass through fearfulness."

There was a noise in the sky that spoke and said:
"Seven terrors are the garments of Huwawa.

The aura of Huwawa is the terrors.
Helpless is he who enters the Cedar Forest

when the demon wears the seven. Hurry, Huwawa
has not put on the seven. He wears but one."

ii

They came to the Cedar Forest that grew upon
the sides of the Cedar Mountain, throne of Irnini,

forbidden dwelling place of immortal gods.
This was the place the guardian demon guarded

to frighten away the daring mortal who
would venture there. But who would venture there?

This was the place Huwawa was; Huwawa's
breath is death. Beautiful is the Forest;

green upon green the cedars; fragrant the air
with the fragrance of cedar trees; the box that grew

along the silent walks of the guardian demon,
shadowed and still, utterly still, was fragrant.

Then Gilgamesh was afraid, and Enkidu
was afraid, and they entered into the Forest, afraid,

the two of them together, and felled some cedars.
The guardian of the Cedar Forest roared.

Then followed confusions of voices and also of hearts.
"The life of man is short." "Helpless is he

who enters the Forest." "Protect us as we pass
through fearfulness." "Where is the strength, the courage?"

Always the face of Huwawa was somewhere there.
There was the noise of swords, daggers, and axes,

confusions of noises in the Cedar Forest.
Then Gilgamesh saw the face of Huwawa the demon

and fled from the face, hiding himself away,
and Enkidu found him and said: "Two people, companions,

they can prevail together against the terror."
There was the noise of swords, daggers, and axes,

confusions of noises in the Cedar Forest.
Always the face of Huwawa was somewhere there.

The guardian of the Forest roared, and then
the companions fought each other in the confusions

of hearts, confusions of noises, swords, and axes.
Then Enkidu saw the face of Huwawa the demon

and fled from the face, hiding himself away,
and Gilgamesh found him and said: "Two people, companions,

they can prevail together against the terror."
Then Gilgamesh said: "The face of Huwawa keeps changing!"

Enkidu said: "You are the strongest of all."
Gilgamesh, weeping, cried out to the god Shamash:

"Protect us as we pass through fearfulness."
Then Shamash heard the prayer of Gilgamesh

and raised up thirteen storms against Huwawa;
the Wind of Simurru and the North Wind and the South

Wind and the West Wind and the East Wind and the Bone-
Cold Wind and the Great Storm Wind and the Great Snow Wind

and the Ice Wind and the Sand Wind and the Screaming
Wind and the Devil Wind and the Bad Wind;

he raised up thirteen storms to beat against
the face of the aura of the demon Huwawa,

beating their tempest feet upon the earth
and breaking the earth wide open, splitting the mountains,

lightning and thunder revolving everywhere.
Then Gilgamesh was able to get at him.

iii

Huwawa spoke and said to Gilgamesh:
"I will cut down the trees for you. Make me your servant.

Shamash has sent you upon this errand against me.
You are the child of the Lady Wildcow Ninsun.

You are the king in Uruk. I will be guardian
of the wood to build the gates of the city of Uruk."

Enkidu spoke and said to Gilgamesh:
"Do not listen to the demon. He must be killed,

obliterated utterly. Listen to me."
Huwawa said: "Do not listen to him who has

neither father nor mother, child of the wilderness.
When Enlil hears of this, the first of gods,

the god of the wilderness, Enkidu knows
that there will be a curse because of this."

Enkidu said: "The demon must be killed
before Enlil and the other gods are told.

Huwawa must be killed and you must build
out of the wood of the tallest cedar a gate,

a gate for the city, a great monument telling
how Gilgamesh slew the guardian of the Forest."

Then the two of them together seized the demon
and by the tongue pulled all his insides out,

and so he died. Then Gilgamesh built the gate
made from the cedar taller than all the rest

of the cedar trees that grew in the Cedar Forest.
They built a raft and they floated the gate to the city.

Enkidu steered the raft and Gilgamesh carried
the head of Huwawa, the guardian of the Forest.

TABLET VI

i

When Gilgamesh the king came back to the city
after the victory over the demon Huwawa,

he washed the filth of battle from his hair
and washed the filth of battle from his body,

put on new clothes, a clean robe and a cloak
tied with a sash, and cleaned and polished the weapons

that had been bloody with the hateful blood
of the demon Huwawa, guardian of the Forest,

and put a tiara on his shining hair,
so that he looked as beautiful as a bridegroom.

The goddess Ishtar saw him and fell in love
with the beauty of Gilgamesh and longed for his body.

"Be my lover, be my husband," she spoke and said.
"Give me the seed of your body, give me your semen;

plant your seed in the body of Ishtar.
Abundance will follow, riches beyond the telling:

a chariot of lapis lazuli
and brass and ivory, with golden wheels,

and pulled, instead of mules, by storm beasts harnessed.
Enter our house: from floor and doorpost breathes

the odor of cedar; the floor kisses your feet.
Princes and kings bow down to offer their wealth,

the best of the yield of orchard, garden, and field.
Your doe goats give you triplets, your ewes also;

your chariot steeds and oxen beyond compare."
Gilgamesh answered and said: "What could I offer

the queen of love in return, who lacks nothing at all?
Balm for the body? The food and drink of the gods?

I have nothing to give to her who lacks nothing at all.
You are the door through which the cold gets in.

You are the fire that goes out. You are the pitch
that sticks to the hands of the one who carries the bucket.

You are the house that falls down. You are the shoe
that pinches the foot of the wearer. The ill-made wall

that buckles when time has gone by. The leaky
waterskin soaking the waterskin carrier.

Who were your lovers and bridegrooms? Tammuz the slain,
whose festival wailing is heard, year after year,

under your sign. He was the first who suffered.
The lovely shepherd bird whom Ishtar loved,

whose wing you broke and now wing-broken cries,
lost in the darkness on the forest floor:

'My wing is broken, broken is my wing.'
The lion whom you loved, strongest of beasts,

the mightiest of the forest, who fell into
the calamity of the pits, the bewildering

contrivances of the goddess, seven times seven.
You broke the great wild horse and snaffled him:

he drinks the water his hobbled hooves have muddied.
The goatherd who brought you cakes and daily for you

slaughtered a kid, you turned him into a wolf
chased away by the herdsmen, whose hairy flanks,

smelly and mangy, the guardian dogs snap at.
You loved Ishullanu, your father's gardener,

who brought you figs and dates to adorn your table.
You looked at him and showed yourself to him

and said: 'Now, touch me where you dare not, touch me
here, touch me where you want to, touch me here.'

He said: 'Why should I eat the rotten food,
having been taught to eat the wholesome food?

Why should I sin and be cursed and why should I live
where the cold wind blows through the reeds upon the outcast?'

Some say the goddess turned him into a frog
among the reeds, with haunted frog voice chanting,

beseeching what he no longer knows he longs for;
some say into a mole whose blind foot pushes

over and over again against the loam
in the dark of the tunnel, baffled and silent, forever.

And you would do with me as you did with them."

ii

Ishtar was enraged and went to the gods in heaven,
to Anu her father and to her mother Antum.

"The king of Uruk has insulted me.
He has found out and told about my foulness."

Anu her father said to the goddess then:
"Why do you rage? Was it not you who longed

for the semen of Gilgamesh? Was it not you
who desired his body? Why then do you rage?

He has found out and told about your foulness."
The goddess said to the god her father thus:

"Give me the Bull of Heaven that I may punish
Gilgamesh the king, who has found out

and told about the foulness of the goddess.
Give me the Bull of Heaven with which to kill him.

Give me the Bull of Heaven or I will go
to the Underworld and break its doors and let

the hungry dead come out to eat the living.
How many are the dead compared to the living!"

Then Anu her father god said to the goddess:
"If I should give the Bull of Heaven to you,

then there would follow seven years of husks.
Have you prepared for this? Have there been garnered

grasses and grain to help sustain the people?"
Ishtar replied to the god her father thus:

"I have prepared for this, for I have garnered
grasses and grain to help sustain the people

during the time of seven years of husks."

iii

So Anu gave the Bull of Heaven to her,
and it came down from heaven snorting and bellowing.

Euphrates shook. The city of Uruk shook
and the earth broke open under the great bull noise.

One hundred men of Uruk fell in the pit
and died in the pit the bellowing broke open.

The Bull of Heaven bellowed and Uruk shook,
Euphrates shook, and the earth broke open again.

One hundred men of Uruk fell in the hole
the great bull noise broke open, and died in the hole.

For the third time the Bull of Heaven bellowed
and Uruk shook; and Enkidu fought the Bull

and took hold of the Bull by the horns and the great bull head
thrashed over him and the reeking bull slobber poured

over his face and Enkidu fought the Bull
and the foul tail of the Bull brushed over his face

and Enkidu wrestled and Enkidu cried out
to Gilgamesh: "The life of man is short,

let us contend with the Bull of Heaven, and win,"
and Gilgamesh fought, and fighting the Bull they cried:

"Two people, companions, they can prevail together,"
and Enkidu seized the Bull by the reeking tail

and Gilgamesh thrust his sword with the skill of a butcher
between the shoulders and horns, and they killed the Bull.

They tore out the great bull heart and offered the heart
to Shamash, bowing before the god, two brothers.

After the battle the two sat down and rested.

iv

Then Ishtar was enraged and the goddess climbed
the parapet of the city of Uruk

and spoke her curse: "Woe be to Gilgamesh
for insult to Ishtar, for Gilgamesh

found out and told the foulness of the goddess,
and killed the Bull of Heaven which Anu sent

in punishment from heaven to shake the city."
Then Enkidu was enraged against the goddess.

He seized a haunch of the slaughtered Bull of Heaven
and tore it loose and flung it toward the wall

on which the goddess stood, and said to her:
"If I could reach you I would do to you

what you have seen me do to the Bull of Heaven.
I would festoon you with the guts of the Bull."

Ishtar went to her temple and with her maidens,
the votaries, and the temple prostitutes,

did ritual mourning over the haunch of the Bull.
But Gilgamesh gathered the craftsmen of the city

to show them the wonderful Bull and how it was made:
the great horns of lapis lazuli,

the coating on the horns two fingers thick.
He cut off the horns and filled the horns with oil,

six measures of oil, and then he offered the oil
in homage to his father, Lugalbanda;

he carried the horns to his chamber in the palace
and hung them in the chamber as a trophy.

Then Gilgamesh and Enkidu together
went hand in hand, two brothers, to the Euphrates,

and washed their hands in the calm river waters.
The people of the city gathered to bless them

and watch them in their progress through the streets.
Gilgamesh spoke and said: "I am the strongest.

My fame will be secure to all my sons.
The city scorns the goddess and shouts in praise

of Gilgamesh because he has won the glory."
That night there was dancing and singing in the palace

in celebration of the victory.
But afterwards, when all had fallen asleep,

Enkidu had a dream and he awakened
to tell the dream to Gilgamesh the king.

"Why is it that the gods are meeting in council?"

i

"I dreamed that the gods were offended and held a council,
and Anu said: 'They have killed the Bull of Heaven

and killed Huwawa. One of them must die,
the one of them who felled the tallest cedar.'

Then Enlil said that Enkidu must die
but Gilgamesh, the gifted, must not die.

And Shamash said: 'The two of them went together,
companions on my errand into the Forest.

Why then should Enkidu, who went, companion,
into the Cedar Forest on my errand,

why should he die?' Angry Enlil said:
'You went with them as if *you* were companion,

day after day as they went upon their journey
to violate the Forest and kill the guardian.' "

ii

And so it was that Enkidu fell sick.
Gilgamesh looked at him and weeping said:

"Why am I left to live while my brother dies?
Why should he die and I be spared to live?"

Enkidu said: "Must I now go to sit
among the dead, in the company of the dead

without my brother?" Gilgamesh said: "Must I
now sit outside the door of the house of the dead

while Enkidu sits in the house of the dead among
the shadow companions?" Then Enkidu cursed the portal

made of the cedar tree they had felled in the Forest:
"You stupid wooden door that does not hear.

I searched for twenty leagues to find the cedar,
tallest of all, with which to make a great

monument for the city, suitable
to celebrate the story of the famous

victory in the Forest over the guardian.
If I had known that this would happen to me

I would have taken my ax and chopped to bits
the wood of the cedar I helped bring to the city.

Grant that some future king destroy the portal
or that a god obliterate from it

utterly the name of Enkidu.
May the name of the companion be forgotten."

Gilgamesh listened to him and weeping said:
"The stormy heart of Enkidu the companion

rages with understanding of the fate
the high gods have established for mankind.

To rage against the gods of heaven is futile.
What Enlil has ordained cannot be changed.

This is the truth told in the frightening dream.
Gilgamesh the brother will pray to the gods,

beseeching the high gods to spare the companion;
Gilgamesh the king will build a statue

to celebrate the fame of Enkidu."

iii

In the early hours of the next morning dawning,
Enkidu, sleepless, weeping, cried out to Shamash:

"As for the hunter who saw me in the grasslands,
may the creatures which he hunts, the gazelles and the others,

get away from him free. May the hunter starve
because he saw me at the watering place.

Fill in his hunting pits, unset his traps,
so that he can no longer be a hunter."

With the first light of the early morning dawning,
Enkidu, sleepless, cried out against the harlot:

"As for the harlot who brought me to the city,
this is the curse of Enkidu against her:

May the garbage of the city be what you eat.
May you drink what flows along the alley gutters.

May you importune in the alley shadows.
May you have no home. May you sleep on the city doorsteps.

May there be signs of vomit on your clothes.
May all men curse and revile you and turn away.

Because of you the creatures fled from me,
who dwelt with them and ranged the hills with them."

Then Shamash spoke and said to Enkidu:
"Why do you curse the temple prostitute?

Because of her you eat the food and drink
the palace affords. Because of her you wear

the garments suitable for a prince to wear;
you sit in the place of honor nearest the king;

the great ones of the earth bow down before you.
Gilgamesh is your friend and your companion.

The grief of Gilgamesh for you will be
the cause of woe and wailing in the city.

Gilgamesh the king will build a statue
to celebrate the fame of Enkidu.

When you are gone, then Gilgamesh will wear
the skins of beasts and hairy-bodied wander

grieving in the wilderness for you."
Enkidu heard what Shamash said to him,

and for a time his stormy heart was quiet.
He repented the curse and blessed the harlot, saying:

"This is the blessing of Enkidu on Shamhat:
May no man revile or curse or turn away.

May the old man comb his locks and beard to please you.
May the young unbuckle his belt in joy for you.

May your house be full of gifts, crystal and gold,
carnelian and lapis lazuli,

earrings and filigree ornaments, fine new clothes.
May the priests invite you with honor into the temple."

iv

In the early hours of the next morning dawning,
Enkidu lay in his bed, fear in his belly.

He told a dream to Gilgamesh who was there.
"I had a dream. There was a noise in the sky

and a noise in the earth in answer. On a dark plain
I was alone. But there was one, a man,

with a lion head, and the paws of a lion too,
but the nails were talons, the talons of an eagle.

The face was dark. He took hold of me and seized me.
I fought with him, I hit at him, but he

kept moving about in the dark, too quick for me,
and then with a blow he capsized me like a raft.

I cried out in the dark to Gilgamesh,
'Two people, companions,' but the man overpowered me,

and raged like a wild bull over me in glory,
and Gilgamesh was afraid and did not help me.

Then I was changed into something like a bird,
with a bird's arms, as spindly as a bird's,

and feathered like a bird. He seized an arm
and led me to the dwelling of Irkalla,

the House of Darkness, the House of No Return.
No one comes back who ever enters there.

The garments that they wear are made of feathers.
The food they eat is clay, the drink is dirt.

Stillness and dust are on the door and door bolt.
There is no light of any sort at all.

Dead kings were there, and princes of old kingdoms,
dead high priests and acolytes were there,

dead chanters and anointers, bearers of ointments;
Etana was there and Sumuqan was there,

and on her throne Ereshkigal the Queen
of the Underworld, and kneeling before her was

Belit-Seri the Scribe who holds the tablet
on which the fate of everyone is written.

She turned her head and looked at us and said:
'Who has led here this latest to arrive?' "

Gilgamesh said: "The dream is terrible."
Enkidu said: "We went together through

the dangers of the Forest and we killed
the Bull of Heaven. Do not forget how we,

two people together, prevailed against the terror."
Enkidu lay suffering on the bed of terror

another day and another day and another,
and the long nights between, and day after day

the suffering of Enkidu grew worse.
On the twelfth day he raised up in his bed

and spoke these words to Gilgamesh and said:
"Gilgamesh, who encouraged me in the battle,

saying, 'Two people, companions, they can prevail,'
Gilgamesh is afraid and does not help me!"

After that Gilgamesh heard the death rattle.

TABLET VIII

With the first light of the early morning dawning,
in the presence of the old men of the city,

Gilgamesh, weeping, mourned for Enkidu:
"It is Enkidu, the companion, whom I weep for,

weeping for him as if I were a woman.
He was the festal garment of the feast.

On the dangerous errand, in the confusions of noises,
he was the shield that went before in the battle;

he was the weapon at hand to attack and defend.
A demon has come and taken away the companion.

He ranged the hills together with the creatures
whose hearts delight to visit the watering places.

A demon has come and taken him away.
He was the first to find the way through the passes

to go to the Cedar Forest to kill Huwawa.
He sought the wilderness places to find the water

with which to quench our thirst on the way to the Forest.
Together we killed Huwawa; together we fought

the bellowing Bull of Heaven, and killed the Bull,
and together the two of us sat down to rest.

Then a demon came and took away the companion.
You are asleep. What has taken you into your sleep?

Your face is dark. How was your face made dark?"
Enkidu's eyes were unmoving in their sockets.

Gilgamesh touched the heart of the companion.
There was nothing at all. Gilgamesh covered

Enkidu's face with a veil like the veil of a bride.
He hovered like an eagle over the body,

or as a lioness does over her brood.

ii

With the first light of the early morning dawning,
Gilgamesh said to Enkidu the companion:

"May the wild ass in the mountains braying mourn.
May the furtive panthers mourn for Enkidu,

the gazelles and the other grazing creatures mourn
for Enkidu at the wilderness watering places.

May the pathways to the Cedar Forest mourn.
May the passes through the mountains mourn for you.

May the old men of the city mourn, and those
who warned and blessed us on our journey mourn.

May the grasslands wail as if they were your mother.
May the gazelle your mother and the wild ass

your father mourn for Enkidu their child.
The milk you were suckled on was the milk of the creatures,

and the creatures taught you to graze in the wild pastures.
May the holy river mourn, the river Ulaja;

Euphrates mourn whose pure river waters
we made libations of, and drank the waters.

May the young men of the city who fought the Bull,
may they mourn for Enkidu who protected them.

May the farmer who sings of you as he works in the field
mourn as he works in the field, may the shepherds mourn,

who brought you the beer and the cooked food in their camp,
may they mourn for you because you protected them

so that they slept at night in peaceful sleep.
May the harlot weep for you who showed you her body

and showed you the things a woman knows how to do.
May the priests mourn in the rite of lamentation.

Listen to me, you elders of the city,
it is Enkidu, the companion, whom I weep for."

iii

Gilgamesh called together the makers of statues,
lapidaries, forgers, workers in copper and gold,

and commanded that there be made a statue of him,
of Enkidu the companion, to honor his deeds.

And Gilgamesh spoke to Enkidu's memory, saying:
"You wore the garments suitable for a prince.

You sat in the place of honor nearest the king.
The great ones of the earth bowed down before you.

Gilgamesh was your friend and your companion.
Gilgamesh the king has built a statue

to celebrate the fame of Enkidu.
The grief of Gilgamesh for you has been

the cause of woe and wailing in the city.
Now you are gone, and Gilgamesh will wear

the skins of beasts and wander hairy-bodied
grieving in the wilderness for you."

With the first light of the early morning dawning,
he made an altar and on the altar offered,

in a carnelian bowl, an offering
of honey, and in another bowl, of lapis

lazuli made, an offering of butter:
these offerings to propitiate the god.

TABLET IX

i

Gilgamesh wandered in the wilderness
grieving over the death of Enkidu

and weeping saying: "Enkidu has died.
Must I die too? Must Gilgamesh be like that?"

Gilgamesh felt the fear of it in his belly.
He said to himself that he would seek the son

of Ubartutu, Utnapishtim, he,
the only one of men by means of whom

he might find out how death could be avoided.
He said to himself that he would hasten to him,

the dangers of the journey notwithstanding.

ii

At night in the mountain passes there were lions,
and Gilgamesh was afraid, and entered afraid

into the moonlit mountain passes, praying
to Sin the moon god: "Hear my prayer and save me

as I enter into the passes where there are lions!"
At night when he lay down to sleep there were

confusions of dreams and in the dreams confusions
of noises, confusions of swords, daggers, axes.

An adversary gloried over him
in struggle, and in the dream who knows who won?

iii

Gilgamesh came to the mountain called Mashu,
whose great twin heads look one way and the other:

the one looks toward the setting of the sun;
the other toward the rising of the sun.

The great twin heads brush up against the Heavens;
the great udders of the mountain hang down into

the shadows of the Cavern of the Earth.
Twin Dragon Scorpion Beings whose look is death

are the guardians of the entrance into the mountain.
The aura of the demon guardian Beings

shimmers across the surface of the mountain.
The shimmering of the light is death to look at.

The Male Twin Monster Being said to the Female:
"Who is it dares come here must be a god."

The Female Twin Monster Being said to her husband:
"Two-thirds a god. The third part is mortal."

Terror in the body of Gilgamesh
seized hold of him from within and held him there

in terror. But then, in terror, he went forward.
Then the Male Dragon Being said to him:

"Who is it dares come here? Why have you journeyed
through fearful wilderness making your way through dangers

to come to this mountain no mortal has ever come to?"
Gilgamesh answered, his body seized in terror:

"I come to seek the father, Utnapishtim,
who was admitted to the company

of gods, who granted him eternal life.
I come to seek the answer to the question

that I must ask concerning life and death."
The Scorpion Monster Being said to him:

"No mortal has ever journeyed through the mountain.
This is the path of the sun's journey by night.

Lightless the sun utterly lightless goes
from the setting to the rising through the mountain.

This is the path of the sun, utterly dark,
twelve leagues of darkness through, utterly lightless.

No mortal would ever be able to go this way."
Gilgamesh said, his body seized in terror:

"This is the way that Gilgamesh must go,
weeping and fearful, struggling to keep breathing,

whether in heat or cold, companionless.
Open the gate to the entrance into the mountain."

Monster Husband and Wife murmured together.
Then the Male Twin Monster said to Gilgamesh:

"The gate to the entrance into the mountain is open.
May Gilgamesh in safety make the journey."

After the Scorpion Dragon Being spoke,
Gilgamesh went to the entrance into the mountain

and entered the darkness alone, without a companion.
By the time he reached the end of the first league

the darkness was total, nothing behind or before.
He made his way, companionless, to the end

of the second league. Utterly lightless, black.
There was nothing behind or before, nothing at all.

Only, the blackness pressed in upon his body.
He felt his blind way through the mountain tunnel,

struggling for breath, through the third league, alone,
and companionless through the fourth, making his way,

and struggling for every breath, to the end of the fifth,
in the absolute dark, nothing behind or before,

the weight of the blackness pressing in upon him.
Weeping and fearful he journeyed a sixth league,

and, blind, to the end of the seventh league, alone,
without a companion, seeing nothing at all,

weeping and fearful, struggling to keep breathing.
At the end of the eighth league he cried aloud

and tried to cry out something against the pressure
of blackness: "Two people, who are companions, they . . . !"

There was nothing behind or before him in the darkness;
utterly lightless, the way of the sun's night journey.

He struggled to breathe, trying to breathe the darkness.
He was weeping and fearful, alone, without a companion.

Just then, at the end of the ninth league, just once
the rough tongue of the North Wind licked at his face.

It was like the tongue of a wild bull or a lion.
He struggled on through darkness, trying to breathe.

The darkness pressed in upon him, both nothing and something.
After he struggled, blind, his companionless way

through eleven leagues of the darkness, nothing at all
and something, ahead of him, a league ahead

a little light, a grayness, began to show.
Weeping and fearful, struggling to keep breathing,

he made his way through the last league of the journey,
twelve leagues in the darkness, alone, companionless,

weeping and fearful, struggling to keep breathing,
he made his way and finally struggled out free

into the morning air and the morning sunlight.

He emerged from the mountain into a wonderful garden.
Gilgamesh looked at the garden and wondered at it.

The fruit and foliage of the trees were all
the colors of the jewels of the world,

carnelian and lapis lazuli,
jasper, rubies, agate, and hematite,

emerald, and all the other gems the earth
has yielded for the delight and pleasure of kings.

And beyond the garden Gilgamesh saw the sea.

TABLET X

i

Veiled Siduri, a tavern keeper, keeps
a tavern on the shore of the glittering sea.

They have given a golden mixing bowl to her
and an ale flagon. She gazed along the shore;

she gazed and gazed and saw that there was coming
along the shore a hairy-bodied man,

a wanderer, who was wearing an animal skin,
coming toward her tavern along the shore.

It was Gilgamesh approaching, two-thirds a god,
but one-third mortal and grieving in his heart.

He looked like one who has undergone a journey,
his face bitten by hunger or by sorrow.

"Who is this man," she said to herself, "who is it,
hairy-bodied, wearing the skin of a beast,

coming toward my tavern along the shore,
looking like one who has undergone a journey,

his face bitten by hunger or by sorrow?"
She was afraid, and shut the door to her tavern,

and slid the door bolt to, and locked the door.
Gilgamesh heard the sound of the door shutting

and heard the sound of the door bolt sliding to.
He called to the tavern keeper: "Tavern keeper,

why have you shut the door against me so?
If you do not let me in I will break the lock

and break the door that shuts me out of the tavern.
It is I who killed the lions in the passes.

It is Gilgamesh, who killed the demon guardian,
Huwawa the guardian of the Cedar Forest.

It is I, who wrestled the Bull of Heaven and killed him.
My fame will be secure to all my sons."

Siduri spoke to Gilgamesh and said:
"If you are Gilgamesh who killed the demon,

and if you killed the lions in the passes,
and if it is you who wrestled the Bull and killed him,

why do you look like one who has undergone
a terrible journey, why do you look like one

who grieves, why do you wear the skin of a beast,
why is it that you roam the wilderness?"

Gilgamesh spoke to the tavern keeper and said:
"I look like one who has undergone a journey,

like one whose grief lives in his heart, and I wander
the wilderness wearing the skin of a beast because

I grieve for the death of Enkidu the companion,
he who has fought with lions and with wolves.

Together we made the journey across the mountains
through the dangerous passes to the Cedar Forest;

he found the secret places where there was water;
together we slew Huwawa the guardian demon;

we fought the Bull of Heaven together and killed him.
Enkidu, the companion, whom I loved,

who went together with me on the journey
no one has ever undergone before,

now Enkidu has undergone the fate
the high gods have established for mankind.

Seven days and nights I sat beside the body,
weeping for Enkidu beside the body,

and then I saw a worm fall out of his nose.
Must I die too? Must Gilgamesh be like that?

It was then I felt the fear of it in my belly.
I roam the wilderness because of the fear.

Enkidu, the companion, whom I loved,
is dirt, nothing but clay is Enkidu.

Weeping as if I were a woman I roam
the paths and shores of unknown places saying:

'Must I die too? Must Gilgamesh be like that?' "
Then veiled Siduri replied to Gilgamesh:

"Who is the mortal who can live forever?
The life of man is short. Only the gods

can live forever. Therefore put on new clothes,
a clean robe and a cloak tied with a sash,

and wash the filth of the journey from your body.
Eat and drink your fill of the food and drink

men eat and drink. Let there be pleasure and dancing."
But Gilgamesh replied to the tavern keeper:

"Tell me the way to find the only one
of men by means of whom I might find out

how death can be avoided. Tell me the way.
What are the signs of the way to Utnapishtim?

If I must cross the sea, I will cross the sea.
If not, I will wander in unknown places, seeking."

The tavern keeper replied to Gilgamesh:
"Not from the beginning of time has anyone ever

been able to go across the glittering sea.
Shamash alone, the Sun, crosses the sea.

He is the only one. Nobody else.
The waters are treacherous, crossing the waters is fearful,

and far out in the waters, forbidding the way,
there slide the other waters, the waters of death.

Urshànabi the boatman dwells out there,
on an island out there somewhere in the waters.

What will you do if you get as far as his island?
He guards the Stone Things and he searches out,

there in the island forest, the Urnu-Snakes.
What will you do if you get to his far-off island,

far out in the treacherous waters? Let Urshànabi
look at the face of Gilgamesh. Perhaps

he will take you with him across the waters of death;
if not, then Gilgamesh must abandon the crossing."

ii

After he crossed the treacherous glittering waters
as far as the island where Urshànabi was,

Gilgamesh raised his ax and drew out his dagger
and entered the island forest. He got to the place

where the Stone Things were, and fell upon them and broke them.
The boatman in the forest heard the noises

of dagger and ax; there was confusion of battle.
Gilgamesh fought a wingèd adversary

that gloried over him in the confusion.
Then Gilgamesh pinioned the wings of the adversary.

He took the broken Stone Things and stowed them away,
together in the boat with the Urnu-Snakes.

Urshànabi the boatman said to him:
"Your face is bitten by hunger or by sorrow.

Why do you look like one who has undergone
a terrible journey? Why do you look like one

who grieves? Why do you wear the skin of a beast?
Why is it that you roam the wilderness?"

And Gilgamesh replied then to the boatman:
"I look like one who has undergone a journey,

like one whose grief lives in his heart, and I wander
the wilderness wearing the skin of a beast because

I grieve for the death of Enkidu the companion,
he who has fought with lions and with wolves.

Together we made the journey across the mountains
through the dangerous passes to the Cedar Forest;

born in the wilderness, Enkidu made a shelter
against the winds that blew across the mountains;

together we slew Huwawa the guardian demon;
we fought the Bull of Heaven together and killed him.

Enkidu, the companion, whom I loved,
who went together with me on the journey

no one has ever undergone before,
now Enkidu has undergone the fate

the high gods have established for mankind.
Seven days and nights I sat beside the body,

weeping for Enkidu beside the body,
and then I saw a worm fall out of his nose.

I roam the wilderness because of the fear.
Enkidu, the companion, whom I loved,

is dirt, the companion Enkidu is clay.
Must I die too? Must Gilgamesh be like that?"

Gilgamesh spoke and said then to the boatman:
"Tell me the way to find the only one

of men by means of whom I might find out
how death can be avoided. Tell me the way.

What are the signs of the way to Utnapishtim?
If I must cross the waters of death, I will.

If not, I will wander in unknown places, seeking."
Urshànabi replied to Gilgamesh:

"With your own hands you have made the crossing harder.
You broke the talismans, you broke the Stone Things;

you took the Urnu-Snakes, which is forbidden.
Take up your ax, go back into the forest.

Cut sixty poles and then cut sixty more,
each pole of sixty cubits; fit them with rings

to strengthen them for poling; find pitch
to seal the wood against the waters of death.

When you have finished, bring me back the poles."
So Gilgamesh went back into the forest,

cut sixty poles and then cut sixty more,
banded the poles, and sealed them against the waters,

and then brought back to the boatman what he had made.
Then Gilgamesh and Urshànabi embarked

on the little boat and made the perilous journey,
by the third day sailing as far as would have been

a two months' sail for an ordinary boat.
And they arrived at the place of the waters of death.

Urshànabi then said to Gilgamesh:
"Let us make our way using the punting poles.

Be sure your hands touch nothing of the water."
So Gilgamesh took up a punting pole

to pole the little boat through the waters of death,
and after a time the wooden pole was broken

because of the might of Gilgamesh the king
poling the little boat through the deadly waters.

And so it was with a second pole, and a third,
a fourth pole, a fifth, and a sixth, and a seventh also;

and so it was with sixty poles, and then
with a sixty-first, and sixty-second, and -third,

and a sixty-fourth, and -fifth, through the death waters,
till all the poles were broken because of his might.

Then Gilgamesh stripped himself and as a sail
held up the animal skin he had been wearing,

and so the little boat sailed on the waters.

iv

The old man standing on the faraway shore
gazed at a little boat approaching. He gazed

at a boat approaching across the waters of death,
and wondering said to himself, consulting his heart:

"The Stone Things have been broken, and there is one
other than Urshànabi in the boat.

I gaze and gaze across the waters of death
but I cannot tell who sails in the boat approaching."

v

The old man spoke and said to Gilgamesh:
"Your face is bitten by hunger or by sorrow.

Why do you look like one who has undergone
a terrible journey? Why do you look like one

who grieves? Why do you wear the skin of a beast?
Why is it that you roam the wilderness?"

And Gilgamesh spoke to the old man and said:
"I look like one whose grief lives in his heart,

because of the death of Enkidu the companion.
Together we made the journey across the mountains

through the dangerous passes to the Cedar Forest;
he told me how the dreams were fortunate;

together we made the festal gate of cedar.
We fought the Bull of Heaven together and killed him,

and after we killed the Bull sat down and rested.
Two brothers, we washed our hands in the calm waters.

Enkidu, the companion, whom I loved,
who went together with me on the journey

no one has ever undergone before,
now Enkidu has undergone the fate

the high gods have established for mankind.
I saw the worm drop out of Enkidu's nose.

Must I die too? Must I too be like that?
I wandered the desert seeking Utnapishtim,

he who is called by men the Faraway;
I lived on the flesh of beasts I hunted down,

lions, and tigers, the bear, the hyena, the panther;
I wore the skins of beasts I had hunted down.

There was no sleep for me in the deserts or mountains.
The tavern keeper shut her door against me.

I lay in the dirt as if I were a beast."
The old man spoke and said to Gilgamesh:

"You who were born the son of a goddess mother,
why do you grieve because of a mortal father?

How long does a building stand before it falls?
How long does a contract last? How long will brothers

share the inheritance before they quarrel?
How long does hatred, for that matter, last?

Time after time the river has risen and flooded.
The insect leaves the cocoon to live but a minute.

How long is the eye able to look at the sun?
From the very beginning nothing at all has lasted.

See how the dead and the sleeping resemble each other.
Seen together, they are the image of death.

The simple man and the ruler resemble each other.
The face of the one will darken like that of the other.

The Annunaki gathered in assembly;
Mammetum, Mother Goddess, she was with them.

There they established that there is life and death.
The day of death is set, though not made known."

i

Gilgamesh spoke and said to the old man then:
"When I looked at you I thought that you were not

a man, one made like me; I had resolved
to challenge you as one might challenge a demon,

a stranger-adversary. But now I see
that you are Utnapishtim, made like me,

a man, the one I sought, the one from whom
I might find out how death can be avoided.

Tell me then, father, how it came about
that you were admitted to the company

of gods, who granted you eternal life."
The father Utnapishtim spoke and said:

"I will tell Gilgamesh the king the story;
a secret of the gods I will disclose.

There was an ancient city, Shuruppak—
you know of it—most fortunate of cities,

god-favored, on the banks of the Euphrates.
The gods in heaven decided in their council

to bring the flood down on the fortunate city.
They sat in secret council together, deciding.

Anu was there, the councilor Enlil,
Ninurta of the Silence, and there also

was the god Ennugi, monitor of canals.
And there was Ea, cleverest of the gods.

The voice of Ea telling me the secret
came whispering through the reed walls of my house:

'You reed house walls, listen and hear me whisper;
listen and be attentive to what I tell you.

Utnapishtim, son of Ubartutu,
abandon your house, abandon what you possess,

abandon your house and build a boat instead.
Seek life instead of riches, save yourself.

Take with you, on the boat you build, an instance
of each thing living so that they may be

safe from obliteration in the flood.
Perform the construction of the boat with care.

Let the length of the boat and the width of the boat be equal.
Roof over the boat as the abyss is roofed.'

The whispering voice spoke through the rustling walls:
'You reed house walls, listen and hear what I say.'

I listened and heard and spoke to the whispering voice:
'I hear what you say. What will I tell the others?

What will I tell the old men and the people?'
Ea the god whispered to me, his servant:

'Tell them you can no longer live in the city,
because you are out of favor with Enlil.

The city is the city of Enlil,
and therefore Utnapishtim, whom he hates,

must find another domicile and another
god who will be his patron and protector,

and you have therefore decided to depart
from Shuruppak and seek another home.

Tell them Ea the god will be your patron,
whose domicile is Apsu the abyss.

Under the roof of Apsu is where you go.
As for the city, fortunate Shuruppak,

in the morning dawning, abundance will then rain down:
there will be plenty, a flood of bounty, the city

teeming with heaven's profusion, game birds falling,
fishes unheard-of before in song or story,

tumbling loaves of fresh-baked morning bread;
grain will come showering in from all the grain fields;

a harvest of everything, yes, more than enough.
These are the things to tell the elders and people.'

"In the first hours of the early morning dawning,
all the people came out for the boat-building,

the little children, the weak as well as the strong,
everyone carrying something: asphalt, and oil,

and pitch, the best of timber with which to build.
Day after day I labored building the boat.

Ten times a dozen cubits were the walls;
ten times a dozen cubits was each deck.

There were six decks; the cabin was divided
into nine compartments. I made up the plans;

I drew a picture of them for our guidance.
I hammered the boat together, and plugged the holes

with water plugs to keep the water out.
I made the bitumen pitch in the pitch kiln,

three *sar* of bitumen pitch to caulk the hull
and, to be certain, three *sar* to caulk the inside.

I counted punting poles and put them aboard;
I had the basket bearers stow the supplies

of oil and foodstuffs, everything I needed.
As for the people who came to help in the work

each day was like a New Year's holiday:
I slaughtered sheep and bullocks for their feasting;

for drinking there was wine and beer, plenty,
as if there was a river overflowing.

On the seventh day I finished building the boat.
I opened a bowl of ointment for my hands.

I commanded the loading of everything I owned
that could be carried, silver, and gold, and all

the instances of living things to be
saved from obliteration in the flood;

and all my household people I took with me.
At sunset on that day I launched the boat.

The launching was very hard to manage. It took
much shifting and much maneuvering on the ways

to get the unwieldy boat down into the river,
and two-thirds of its weight under the water

in order to prevent it from capsizing.
As darkness was coming on I heard the god:

'Abundance will rain down, more than enough!
Get yourself inside, and close the hatch!'

I saw the signs of morning in the sky.
'Abundance will rain down, more than enough!'

I got myself inside, and closed the hatch.
To Puzuramurri the caulker, who, outside,

caulked up the hatch with pitch, I gave my house.

iii

"In the early hours of the next morning dawning
there was the noise of Adad in the clouds

that rose and filled the morning sky with blackness.
Shullat the herald of the dread Adad

moved out over the mountains and over the valleys,
bellowing; Hanish the herald of the dread

Adad moved over the plains and over the cities;
everything turned to darkness as to night.

From time to time the Annunaki blazed
terrible light. Then rain came down in floods.

Beneath, the god of the Underworld, Nergal,
broke down his own doorposts and opened the earth.

Ninurta god of chaos and of war
opened the dikes, and other floods burst forth.

The South Wind rushed in flooding over the mountains.
Brother could not see brother in the welter;

none of the gods in heaven could see the earth;
the land was shattered like a shattered pot;

confusions of dread Adad were everywhere.
Terrified gods got themselves up as high

as they could go, nearest the highest heaven,
cringing against the wall like beaten dogs.

Ishtar cried out like a woman in her birth pangs,
the sweet-voiced lady cried: 'The days that were

have now become as featureless as clay
because of what I said when I went to the gods

in heaven, bringing calamity down on those
whom now the sea engulfs and overwhelms,

my children who are now the children of fish.'
The Annunaki sat and wept with her,

the cowering gods wept, covering their mouths.
Six days and nights the storm went on this way,

the South Wind flooding over the mountains and valleys
until the seventh day when the storm birth labor

subsided at last, the flood subsided at last.
I opened the hatch. The daylight touched my face.

I looked outside. Nothing was moving at all.
It looked as flat as a flat clay roof looks flat;

and all the human beings had turned to clay.
I fell to my knees and wept. The tears ran down

the sides of my nose. I wept in the total silence.
I looked outside and looked as far as I could,

trying to find, looking across the world,
something. And then, far off, something was there.

What looked like signs of an island could faintly be seen;
and then the boat was caught and held from under

by the peak rock of a mountain under the water.
It was Mount Nisir the boat was grounded on.

A first day it was held, and a second day;
a third day the boat was held from under,

and a fourth day, and a fifth; a sixth day,
and then on the seventh day I freed a dove.

The dove flew free and flew away from the boat,
seeking a place for its little feet to alight,

and finding none, flew back to the boat to perch.
I freed a swallow then and it flew free

and flew away from the boat, seeking a place
for its little feet to alight, and finding none,

flew back to the boat to find a place to alight.
I freed a raven then and it flew free

and flew away from the boat, and never returned.
It had found a place to alight, and circled about

the place, and alighted, and settled itself, and ate,
and never after that returned to the boat.

Then I set free all the other birds in the boat
and they flew free, scattering to the winds.

"I went ashore and offered a sacrifice.
I poured out a libation; I set out seven

vessels of offerings on a stand, and then
set seven more; I made a fire of wood

of myrtle, wood of cane, and wood of cedar.
I lit the fire. The odor touched the nostrils

of the Igigi gods and gave them pleasure.
I slaughtered a sheep to make a sacrifice;

the gods collected like flies about the altar.
The great goddess progenitrix Ishtar

came down from heaven wearing about her neck
the pendant Anu gave her for her adornment,

of lapis lazuli ornately made.
She said: 'Just as this pendant never shall

forgotten be by the goddess, so the goddess
never will forget calamitous days.

The gods may come to the ritual but forbidden
is the presence of Enlil, by whose command

the flood was peremptorily brought down
on the heads of all my children, engulfing them.'

When the god Enlil came to the sacrifice
he saw the boat, and the sight filled him with rage.

73

He spoke in anger to the gathered gods:
'How is it that one man has saved himself?

No breath of life was meant to be kept safe
from its obliteration in the flood.'

Ninurta opened his mouth and said to the god:
'Ea, the cleverest of the gods, deviser,

let Ea speak and give Enlil his answer.'
Then Ea opened his mouth and said to the god:

'The punishment should always fit the crime.
Let him who has performed an evil act

be punished for that act. Let not the flood
be brought down on the heads of all for what

one man has done; and he who has transgressed,
show pity to him, lest he be cut off

from all his fellows. Better that a lion
should come into the village and prey upon it,

taking a few, than that the flood drown all.
Better a wolf should find its ravening way

into the fold, devouring some, much better
than that the flood turn all that breathes to clay.

Better that famine starve a few of them
than that a harvest of waters obliterate all.

Better that Erra the plague god, better that he
take hold of some, seize them and bear them away

to the Underworld, than that the flood drown all.
I did not tell the secret to the man.

He listened to the wind and guessed the secret.
Let the gods sitting in council now decide

how to reward the wise man for his wisdom.'
The god Enlil then went on board the boat.

He took me by the hand and made me kneel;
he took my wife by the hand and made her kneel.

The god then touched our foreheads, blessing us,
and said: 'You were but human; now you are

admitted into the company of gods.
Your dwelling place shall be the Faraway,

the place which is the source of the outflowing
of all the rivers of the world there are.'

And so they led us to the Faraway,
the place we dwell in now, which is the source

of all the rivers flowing through the world."
Then scornful Utnapishtim said to the king:

"Tell me, who would bring all the gods together
so that for *you* they might in council decide

what your deserving is, that you be granted
admittance into the company of gods?

Let there be now a test of Gilgamesh.
Let him but keep himself awake for a week,

six nights and seven days, to show his worth."
So Gilgamesh sat down to begin the test.

ν

Almost as soon as Gilgamesh the king
sat down to test himself, a mist of sleep,

as ocean mist comes over the shore from the waters,
came over his eyes, and so the strongest slept.

Then Utnapishtim spoke to his wife and said:
"See how this hero sleeps who asks for life.

As ocean mist blows over the land from the waters,
so the mist of sleep comes over the eyes of the king."

The wife of Utnapishtim answered him:
"Touch and awaken him, so that he may

return in safety to his native city,
entering through the gate of his departure."

But Utnapishtim said: "Man is deceitful.
Therefore he will deceive us. Every day,

as he lies sleeping, you must bake a wafer
and place the wafer near him, making a mark

upon the nearby wall for every day
this hero sleeps who seeks eternal life."

She baked a wafer every day, of bread,
for every day that Gilgamesh lay sleeping.

76

The first wafer was dry as dust; the second
only less so than the first; the third

was soggy and rotten; the fourth wafer was white
in the crust; there were spots of mold on the fifth;

the sixth wafer looked almost as if it was fresh;
and the seventh—Gilgamesh started and waked up

as Utnapishtim touched him on the forehead.
Gilgamesh said: "I had almost fallen asleep

when you reached out and touched me and kept me awake."
But Utnapishtim said to Gilgamesh:

"Look at the wafers and look at the marks on the wall:
a mark and a wafer for every day you have slept.

The first wafer is dry as dust; the second
is only less so than the first; the third

is soggy and rotten; the fourth wafer is white
in the crust; there are spots of mold on the fifth;

the sixth wafer looks almost as if it is fresh;
and the seventh—but it is then that you awoke."

Then Gilgamesh said to him: "What shall I do?
Who takes us away has taken hold of me.

Death is in my chamber when I sleep;
and death is there wherever I set foot."

Utnapishtim said to the boatman then:
"Though your delight has been to cross the waters,

the harbor now is closed, the crossing forbidden.
The waters and the shore now shun the boatman.

The hairy-bodied man you brought across
the perilous waters, wearing the skin of a beast

that hides his beauty, let Urshànabi take him
to the washing place. There let him wash his body,

washing away the filth that hides his beauty.
Manifest be the beauty of Gilgamesh.

Take the skin of a beast he wore on the journey
and throw it away in the sea. Let Gilgamesh

bind up his shining hair with a new fillet.
Let him put on a spotless festal robe.

Let him return to his native city in honor
in the royal garments appropriate to himself."

The boatman led the king to the washing place.
Gilgamesh washed his body, washing away

the filth that obscured his beauty; then Urshànabi
took the skin of a beast and threw it away.

Manifest was the beauty of Gilgamesh.
He bound up his shining hair with a new fillet;

he put on a festal robe, utterly spotless,
a royal garment appropriate to himself.

Then he and the boatman boarded the little boat
and the boat began to move away from the shore.

But the wife of Utnapishtim said to her husband:
"This man has undergone a terrible journey.

What will you give him for his return to his city?"
Gilgamesh, hearing, took up his punting pole

and brought the little boat back to the shore.
Utnapishtim spoke and said to him:

"Gilgamesh, you who have made the terrible journey,
what shall I give you for your return to your city?"

Then Utnapishtim said to Gilgamesh:
"A secret of the gods I will disclose.

There is a plant that grows under the waters,
thorny to seize, as a rose is thorny to seize.

How-the-Old-Man-Once-Again-Becomes-a-Young-Man
is the name of the plant that grows under the waters.

Descend into the waters and seize the plant."
So Gilgamesh tied heavy stone weights to his feet

to bring him down through the waters of the abyss
to the place where he could find the magic plant.

He seized the thorny plant that cut his hands;
he cut the stone weights loose from his heavy feet;

and the waters cast him up upon the shore.

vii

Gilgamesh said to Urshànabi the boatman:
"Urshànabi, this plant is a wonderful plant.

New life may be obtained by means of it.
I will carry the thorny plant back to my city.

I will give some of the plant to the elders there,
to share among them, telling them it is called

How-the-Old-Man-Once-Again-Becomes-a-Young-Man.
And I will take my share of the magic plant,

once more to become the one who is youngest and strongest."

viii

At twenty leagues they stopped only to eat;
at thirty leagues they stopped to rest for the night.

Gilgamesh found a spring, a pool of pure water.
He entered the water, to refresh himself.

In the reeds nearby a serpent of the place
became aware of the fragrance of the plant,

breathed its perfume, desired it, and approached,
and stole away with it among the reeds.

As it disappeared the serpent shed its skin.
When Gilgamesh found out what the serpent had done

he sat down weeping by the pool of water.
He took Urshànabi by the hand and said:

"What shall I do? The journey has gone for nothing.
For whom has my heart's blood been spent? For whom?

For the serpent who has taken away the plant.
I descended into the waters to find the plant

and what I found was a sign telling me to
abandon the journey and what it was I sought for."

ix

At twenty leagues they stopped only to eat.
At thirty leagues they stopped to rest for the night.

And so they traveled until they reached Uruk.
There Gilgamesh the king said to the boatman:

"Study the brickwork, study the fortification;
climb the great ancient staircase to the terrace;

study how it is made; from the terrace see
the planted and fallow fields, the ponds and orchards.

One league is the inner city, another league
is orchards; still another the fields beyond;

over there is the precinct of the temple.
Three leagues and the temple precinct of Ishtar

measure Uruk, the city of Gilgamesh."

GILGAMESH, ENKIDU,

AND THE NETHER WORLD

(TABLET XII)

"The Drum and Drumstick I had in the Carpenter's house,
where the Carpenter's daughter was, and the Carpenter's wife—

wife and daughter were like my mother and sister—
the Drum and Drumstick that I had have fallen

down through a hole into the Nether World,
out of my sight, down through a hole in the floor.

Who will bring back my Drumstick from down there?
Who will bring back my Drum from the Nether World?"

Enkidu heard what Gilgamesh was saying,
and said, his servant, then, to Gilgamesh:

"I will bring up the Drumstick from below.
I will bring back the Drum from the Nether World."

Gilgamesh heard the promise of Enkidu,
and with these words he thus admonished him:

"If you go down to the Nether World for me,
listen to what I tell you about your going.

Do not put on clean clothes when you go down there,
or they will know you come down there a stranger.

Do not anoint your body with fragrant oil.
The fragrance will cause them to gather about you like flies.

Carry no staff or bow along with you,
or, startled up, the spirits will flutter around you.

Do not wear shoes when you go to the House of the Dead.
Let not your step be heard on that booming floor.

Refrain from kissing the wife your heart has loved;
refrain from striking the wife your heart has hated;

refrain from kissing the son dear to your heart;
and do not strike the son your heart has shunned;

or you will be seized and held by the Cry of the Dead:
Naked the goddess mother lies in hell;

naked, Ninazu's mother lies exposed,
the holy garment fallen from her shoulders,

bare are the breasts of the mother, Ereshkigal.

ii

Then Enkidu went down to the Nether World
not heeding the admonishments of the king.

He wore clean clothes when he went to the House of the Dead,
and so they knew he came down there a stranger.

He anointed his body with fragrant oil, and they
collected like flies, attracted by the fragrance.

He carried a staff and bow with him when he went.
Startled, the spirits fluttered all around him.

The sounds of the shoes he wore were heard in that place;
the echoing floor of the House of the Dead resounded.

He did not refrain from kissing the wife he loved;
he did not refrain from striking the hated wife;

he embraced and kissed the son who was dear to him;
and did not refrain from striking the hated son.

And so the Cry of the Dead seized him and held him:
Naked the goddess mother lies in hell;

naked, Ninazu's mother lies exposed,
the holy garment fallen from her shoulders,

bare are the breasts of the mother, Ereshkigal.
The Cry of the Dead seized him and held him fast.

Namtar the demon did not seize and hold him.
Ashak the fever demon did not hold him.

Nergal's pitiless viceroy did not seize him.
It was the Cry of the Dead that seized and held him.

He did not fall in battle. It was the Cry.
The Nether World itself it was that seized him;

Ereshkigal the Queen it was who held him.

Gilgamesh grieved for the death of Enkidu.
Grieving he went to the house of the god Enlil.

"Enlil, Father, my Drum fell through the floor
of the Upper World into the Nether World.

I saw my Drumstick fall, out of my sight.
The Cry of the Nether World has seized my servant,

Enkidu, whom I sent to bring me back
the Drum and Drumstick that I had that fell

down through a hole into the Nether World.
Namtar the demon did not seize and hold him.

The fever demon Ashak did not seize him.
Nergal's pitiless viceroy did not hold him.

It was the Cry of the Dead that seized and held him.
He did not fall in battle. It was the Cry.

The Nether World itself it was that seized him;
Ereshkigal the Queen it was who held him.

O Father Enlil, intercede for me."
But Father Enlil would not intercede.

So Gilgamesh went grieving to the moon god.
"O Father Sin, my Drum fell through a hole

in the floor of the Upper World into the Nether.
My Drumstick fell through the hole, I saw it fall.

The Cry has seized my servant, Enkidu,
whom I sent to bring me back from the world down there

the Drum and Drumstick that I had that fell
down through a hole in the floor of the Upper World.

The demon Namtar did not seize and hold him.
Ashak the fever demon did not hold him.

Nergal's pitiless viceroy did not seize him.
It was the Cry of the Dead that seized and held him.

He did not fall in battle. It was the Cry.
The Nether World itself it was that seized him;

Ereshkigal the Queen it was who held him.
I pray that the god of the moon will intercede."

The god of the moon was deaf to what he asked.
Then Gilgamesh went grieving to the edge

of Apsu the abyss, to the god Ea:
"O Father Ea, into the Nether World

my Drum has fallen through a hole; my Drumstick
fell through a hole, down into the world below.

The Cry of the Nether World has seized my servant,
Enkidu, whom I sent to bring me back

the Drum and Drumstick that I had that fell
down through the hole in the floor of the Upper World.

Namtar the demon did not seize and hold him.
Ashak the fever demon did not hold him.

Nergal's pitiless viceroy did not seize him.
It was the Cry of the Dead that seized and held him.

He did not fall in battle. It was the Cry.
The Nether World itself it was that seized him;

Ereshkigal the Queen it was who held him."
The god of the abyss heard what he said,

and interceded for the grieving king.
He said to Nergal, King of the Nether World:

"Open a hole in the roof of the Nether World
so Enkidu may rise up like a vapor

out of the Nether World into the Upper."
Nergal obeyed the voice of Ea the god.

The hole in the floor of the Upper World was open.
The spirit of Enkidu, a puff of breath,

came forth from the Nether World into the Upper.
Then Gilgamesh and Enkidu, companions,

tried to embrace and kiss one another, companions.
Sighing toward one another they spoke these words:

"Now tell me how it is in the Nether World."
"I will not tell you. If I told you how

it is in the Nether World, the arrangement of things,
you would sit down and weep because I told you."

"Now tell me how it is although I may
sit down and weep because of what you tell me."

So Enkidu told him the way it is down there.
"The vermin eat my body that once made

Gilgamesh the companion rejoice to touch;
as if it was old clothes, filthy, discarded,

the vermin eat the body of Enkidu."
Then Gilgamesh cried woe and fell to the ground,

because of the things that Enkidu was telling.

iv

After a time he further questioned him
about the way it is among the dead.

"Have you seen down there the man who has no son?"
"I have seen the sonless man in the Nether World."

"How is it with the man who has one son?"
"I have seen the man. He sits by the wall and weeps."

"Have you seen the man down there who has two sons?"
"He sits on two bricks and has some bread to eat."

"How is it with the man who has three sons?"
"He drinks from the waterskin his sons have brought."

"Have you seen the man down there who has four sons?"
"His heart rejoices as the heart rejoices

of a farmer with four asses yoked to his cart."
"How is it with the man who has five sons?"

"They treat him in the Nether World as if
he were a scribe of the court, dispenser of justice."

"Have you seen down there the man who has six sons?"
"His heart rejoices as the heart rejoices

of one who drives his plow in a rich field."
"How is it with the man with seven sons?"

"As if he were a companion of the gods
he sits upon a throne and listens to music."

"Have you seen the man who fell from the mast and drowned?"
"I have seen the drowned man in the Nether World."

"How is it with the man who suddenly died?"
"They bring pure water to him on his couch."

"Have you seen in the Nether World the famous warrior,
he who fell on the battlefield in glory?"

"The grieving parents raise up the head of the son;
the mourning wife grieves at the couch of death."

"And he whose corpse was thrown away unburied?"
"He wanders without rest through the world down there."

"The one who goes to the Nether World without
leaving behind him any to mourn for him?"

"Garbage is what he eats in the Nether World.
No dog would eat the food he has to eat."

NOTES

I should explain the constraints within which I have worked. I cannot read cuneiform and do not know the language, or languages, the Gilgamesh epic was written in. As my sources and authorities I have used three literal line-by-line translations, first and foremost "The Epic of Gilgamesh," by E. A. Speiser, in *Ancient Near Eastern Texts Relating to the Old Testament* (Princeton University Press, 1969), and two more recent works, *Gilgamesh*, by John Gardner and John Maier (Vintage, 1985), and *The Epic of Gilgamesh*, by Maureen Gallery Kovacs (Stanford University Press, 1989). I have also consulted the excellent prose free version by N. K. Sandars, *The Epic of Gilgamesh* (Penguin, 1972), based on Sumerian as well as Akkadian originals. I did not see the new translation by Stephanie Dalley, *Myths from Mesopotamia: Creation, The Flood, Gilgamesh, and Others* (Oxford World Classics, 1989), in time for my own work to be much affected by it. The new version by Robert Temple, *He Who Saw Everything* (Rider, 1991), is still more recent. I have consulted Jeffrey H. Tigay's *The Evolution of the Gilgamesh Epic* (University of Pennsylvania Press, 1982). I have also read the free-verse free version by Herbert Mason, *Gilgamesh: A Verse Narrative* (Mentor, 1970). While I have tried to avoid borrowing the language of the scholarly translations, I have also tried to use as few expressions as possible which have no authority deriving from one or another of them. (I have pointed out in the notes a few places where I have borrowed an irresistibly telling word or phrase. No doubt there are others.)

Speiser remarks of "Gilgamesh, Enkidu, and the Nether World" (Tablet XII) that "contents and circumstantial evidence mark this tablet as an inorganic appendage to the epic proper." Tablet XII is an Akkadian translation of part of a Sumerian poem and it does seem to me to be different in character from the main poem. To include it as an organic part of the main poem would cause a number of problems, the most obvious of which is that it would spoil the effect of Tablet XI's conclusion, which returns to the language of the opening passage of the poem. I present it therefore as a separate poem, giving it the title conventionally assigned to the Sumerian poem.

There are many gaps in the tablets and therefore in the literal translations, and these gaps have provided both problems and opportunities for me. Tablet I is pretty full, so there is only one line ("Shadow of Darkness over the enemy field") without any authority. Tablets VI and XI are also relatively full, so there are relatively few instances of unauthorized invention by me. In the account of the fight against Huwawa, Tablets IV and V, there are more such instances because there are lots of gaps. This is also true of the opening passages of Tablet IX. These are examples.

There are places where I have exploited scholarly disagreements. Some scholars think that Ishtar, in Tablet VI, turned Ishullanu into a mole; others think he was turned into a frog. I like both possibilities, so I turned the scholars into ancient gossips whose stories, as usual with gossips, don't quite match. Again, this is an example.

There are also places where I have made decisions neither constrained to do so by gaps nor authorized by scholarly disagreements. I have sometimes used expressions in one tablet whose authority can be found only in another. For example, some warrant for my formulation "Two people, companions, they can prevail" can be found in the literal translations of Tablet IV, but I have used it a number of times elsewhere. I have also sometimes condensed somewhat, sometimes expanded a little, sometimes varied the material locally. For example, the literal accounts of Gilgamesh's journey through the sun's nighttime tunnel repeat the same lines over and over; I have invented variations of them, for narrative purposes and to avoid monotony.

Every translation or version of a work is an interpretation of it, because every choice of expression, every metrical decision, is an act of interpretation, and the "true original" is always unrecoverable, even for the most faithfully literal translation. This is all the more obviously the case when the "translator" is not working directly with the original language. So I do not want to make exaggerated claims about faithfulness. But my version tries to be as respectful of the professional scholarship as it is feasible to be.

There is one matter which might cause confusion for the reader who consults the Speiser translation while reading my version. The small Roman numerals between passages in Speiser refer to columns of the tablet in question. My small Roman numerals represent decisions by me about how best to dispose the episodes of the narrative.

The other constraint I have been working in terms of is the verse medium, iambic pentameter lines arranged in unrhymed couplets. My intention has been to obey the laws of this meter as strictly as I could. There are a few places where the line is stretched perhaps beyond its limit ("There is no withstanding the aura or power of the desire"); a few instances of lines with the predicted first syllable omitted ("utterly the name of Enkidu"); a few instances where—one sentence (or clause) ending in the middle of a line and a new one beginning—the space between them is counted as an unspoken syllable (" 'why should he die?' Angry Enlil said").

TABLET I

i. The ancient city of Uruk was situated on the Euphrates, in what is now southern Iraq. Gilgamesh was not actually its founder, but there was a historical Gilgamesh among its earliest Sumerian kings.

Anu is the god of the heavens; Ishtar is the goddess of love and war.

ii. Aruru is a birth goddess.

In my versification "Enkidu" is stressed most strongly on the first syllable, least strongly on the second.

The goddess of grain is Nisaba.

iii. "His face was as one estranged from what he knows." Speiser has "His face was like that of a wayfarer from afar." Gardner-Maier, Kovacs, and Sandars have similar expressions.

iv. I have condensed somewhat the harlot's description here of the city and its pleasures.

Shamash is the sun god. Ea is the god of earth, water, the abyss. Enlil is the god of order, who presides over destinies, comparable perhaps to Zeus.

In Speiser and the other scholarly translations, Gilgamesh has another dream, which I have omitted. It is a dream of an ax but is otherwise similar to the dream of a meteor. Ninsun interprets the two dreams in exactly the same way.

TABLETS II AND III

My rendering here is based mainly on the Speiser translation of Old Babylonian passages. The Assyrian tablets are extremely fragmentary.

i. "She took him by the hand as a goddess might, / leading a worshipper into the temple precinct; / as if he was a child she held his hand." I have taken advantage of alternative possible literal translations of the simile.

iii. "He turned his chest away." I owe this phraseology to the Kovacs translation.

iv. The rendering of this passage follows the Kovacs translation more closely than the others.

v. An alternative name for Huwawa is Humbaba.

TABLETS IV AND V

Tablets IV and V are also fragmentary and the narrative sequence must be pieced together. In my rendering, the dreams occur on the journey of Gilgamesh and Enkidu to the Cedar Forest, and before they arrive there. It seems to me a reasonable arrangement of the narrative. I am relieved to find that this is also the sequence as given in Kovacs (though I had made my own decision before I read her translation). In Speiser, Gardner-Maier, and Sandars, the dreams occur after they have entered the Cedar Forest, though of course before they encounter Huwawa.

Because of the fragmentary condition of the tablets, as reflected in the scholarly translations, there is a good deal of room for local invention, omission, and condensation. For example, there were more dreams recounted on the tablets than I have tried to set forth in detail. The account of the fighting is similarly fragmentary, so there is a good deal of local invention in my rendering.

ii. Irnini is a name for Ishtar.

"Then followed confusions . . ." I have borrowed the useful term "confusions" from Sandars's account, but have made more, and different, use of it than she does. The term is useful to help characterize the nature of the battle and of the emotions of Gilgamesh and Enkidu. Perhaps it also suggests the condition of the original texts.

The wonderful names of the thirteen winds come from the Kovacs translation.

TABLET VI

This tablet, especially in the dialogues between Ishtar and Gilgamesh and between Ishtar and Anu, is less fragmentary than Tablets II–V. But there is necessarily more invention by me toward the end of the tablet, in the account of the battle with the Bull of Heaven and Gilgamesh's triumphant speech after the battle.

i. "Tammuz the slain" is the Babylonian Adonis.

"Some say the goddess turned him into a frog . . . / some say into a mole . . ." I have taken advantage of scholarly disagreements here. Speiser and Sandars say mole; Gardner and Maier say frog, and Kovacs agrees that this may be so.

TABLET VII

The first section and the first five couplets of section ii are based on the literal translations of a Hittite tablet.

iv. Irkalla is a name for the Underworld.

"Etana was there . . ." Etana was an early king. Kovacs has the following note: "The inclusion of Etana in Enkidu's premonition of the Netherworld must be because of some particular relevance of Etana's fate to Enkidu's situation. The fragments of the 'Myth of Etana' tell that Ishtar selected the young Etana to be king, and that he sought the magical 'plant of birth' for his barren wife. An eagle helped him by carrying him up to the heavens, but then fell back to earth."

Relevant to Enkidu's situation, yes, but once one has read Tablet XI, the relevance to Gilgamesh, failed seeker after renewed life, seems even more powerful.

Sumuqan, as mentioned in Tablet I, is the god of cattle.

TABLET VIII

This tablet is very fragmentary. There is a certain amount of local invention in my version, based on what the scholarly translations have put together.

TABLET IX

ii. This part of the original is very fragmentary.

iii. "Mashu" means "twin."

". . . shimmers across the surface of the mountain." This phraseology derives from Speiser.

"Gilgamesh went to the entrance into the mountain . . ." From here to the end of the account of Gilgamesh's journey through the tunnel there is quite a lot of local invention on my part, in this case not so much because of fragmentation as because in the literal translation the lines are extremely repetitious.

TABLET X

i. "The life of man is short. Only the gods / can live forever. Therefore put on new clothes, / a clean robe . . . Eat and drink your fill of the food and drink / men eat and drink. Let there be pleasure and dancing." This passage, which is found only in an Old Babylonian tablet, means roughly what these lines say. But in dealing with it I have appropriated phrases from elsewhere in my own version of the poem. Such transactions between tablets occur also at other places in my treatment.

ii. "Gilgamesh raised his ax and drew out his dagger / and entered the island forest . . ." This episode is extremely fragmentary.

It is not clear exactly what the Stone Things and the Urnu-Snakes are.

v. "How long does a building stand before it falls? . . ." In this passage, Utnapishtim is speaking to Gilgamesh in proverbial language.

The Annunaki are the sons of Anu, gods who preside over one's destiny. Mammetum is another name for Aruru, the birth goddess.

TABLET XI

i. Ninurta is the god of war, as noted in Tablet I.

Ea is god of the abyss, the underground sea, the Hermes or Mercury of these gods.

". . . abundance will then rain down: / there will be plenty, a flood of bounty . . . tumbling loaves of fresh-baked morning bread; / grain will come showering in . . ." I have tried to compensate somewhat for the effect of certain untranslatable puns in the original. As the scholarly translators point out, the word for "bread," for instance, puns on the word for "darkness," the word for "wheat" on the word for "misfortune." I have instead made wordplay with rain and flood words.

ii. Some scholars argue that Puzuramurri was the pilot of the boat and was not left behind. I have taken advantage of scholarly disagreement in order to read the passage with a meaner notion of the character of Utnapishtim.

iii. Adad is the storm god, the thunder-and-lightning god.

Gardner-Maier has the phrase "Brother could not see brother."

Mount Nisir: the Mount Ararat of the biblical account of the Flood.

GILGAMESH, ENKIDU, AND THE NETHER WORLD (TABLET XII)

My version of this poem is based on Speiser's translation in *Ancient Near Eastern Texts* and on the translation by John Gardner and John Maier in their *Gilgamesh*; my version of the questions and answers in section iv is based on Samuel Noah Kramer's translation of the corresponding lines in the Sumerian poem, in "Death and Nether World According to the Sumerian Literary Texts," *Iraq* XX, 67, n. 16.

i. The Akkadian poem begins in the middle of the Sumerian poem of which it is a translation. The meaning of the reference to the Carpenter and his wife and daughter is not clear.

"Carry no staff or bow along with you, / or, startled up, the spirits will flutter around you." I take "flutter" from Kramer's translation of the Sumerian poem.

Ninazu is one of the gods of the Nether World. Ereshkigal is the Queen of the Nether World. Namtar and Ashak are her agents. Nergal is the King of the Nether World.

iv. "After a time he further questioned him, / about the way it is among the dead." There is no authority for this couplet in the scholarly texts. The Akkadian poem is fragmentary at this point.